Peppa Pig™

Peppa Goes Swimming

It's a lovely sunny day and Peppa and her family are at the swimming pool.

"Peppa! George! Let Daddy put on your armbands," snorts Mummy Pig.

Today is George's first time
at the pool and he's a bit
scared of getting in.

"Why don't you just put one foot in the water?" suggests Daddy Pig.
"Maybe George should try both feet at the same time?" says Mummy Pig.

Splash! Mummy Pig convinces George to jump into the water and he loves it!

"Grunt! Hee! Hee! Snort!" shouts George, happily. "Ho! Ho! Well done, George!" snorts Daddy Pig.

Here is Rebecca Rabbit with her brother,
Richard, and their mummy.

"Hello, everyone!"
cries Rebecca.
"Squeak, squeak,"
says Richard.

"Richard, hold on to this float
and you can practise kicking your legs,"
says Mummy Rabbit.

"George, would you like to try
kicking your legs?" asks Mummy Pig.
"Hee! Hee! Float! Snort!" giggles George.

"Big children are very good at swimming," snorts Peppa. "When George and Richard are older, they'll be able to swim like us, won't they, Rebecca?"

"Yes!" says Rebecca, as she watches the boys kicking.

Peppa and Rebecca race each other up and down the pool with their armbands on.

They are having lots of fun swimming
and splashing in the water.

Oops! Richard has dropped his toy
watering can into the pool.
"Mummy! Wah!" cries Richard.
"Sorry, Richard, I can't reach.
It's too far down," says Mummy Rabbit.
Luckily, Daddy Pig is an excellent swimmer.
He takes off his glasses and dives down to get it.

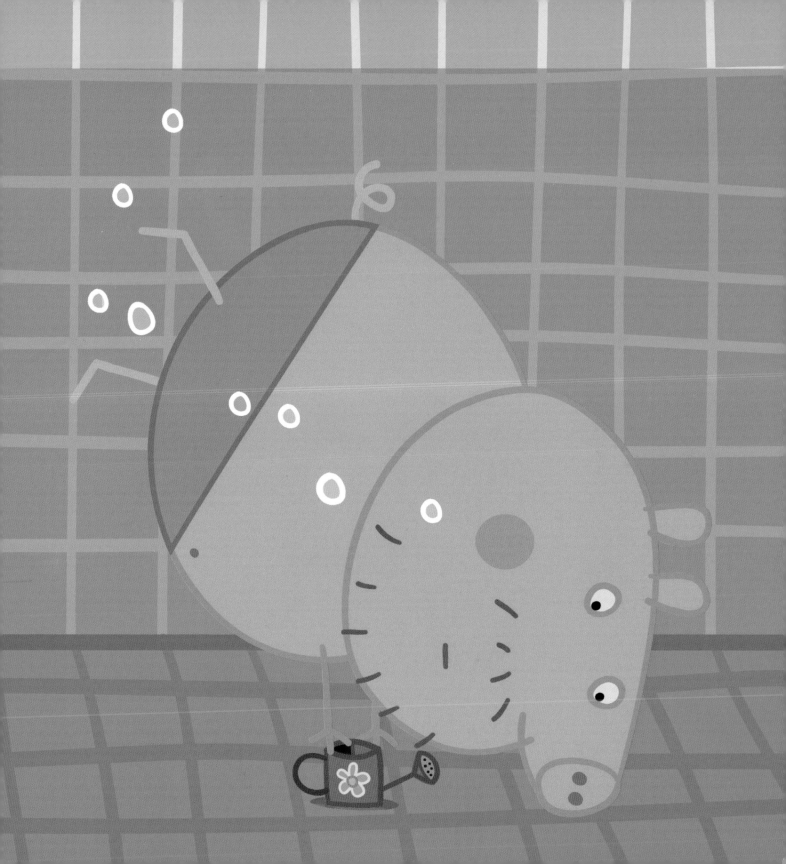

"Ho! Ho! There you go!"
snorts Daddy Pig.
"Squeak, squeak!" says Richard.

"Well done, Daddy!"
smiles Mummy Pig.

dear! Now Richard is soaking Daddy Pig with the watering can. What a naughty Rabbit! "Hee! Hee! Hee!" George thinks it's hilarious. Everyone has had a wonderful day at the pool!